kv

150 Tips for Living, Traveling, and Having Fun in an RV

John Campbell

Table of Contents

Introduction

I would like to truly thank you for buying my book, "RV: 150 Tips for Living, Traveling, and Having Fun in an RV."

This book contains proven steps and strategies on how to live, travel, and have fun in an RV.

Living in an RV is an exciting experience. After all, what could beat living on the road, moving as you desire, and visiting every place you fancy? Despite the joy that comes with living on the road, in order to truly enjoy yourself, you will need to know a few things about RV living. If you want to learn how to truly have fun, then this is the right book for you.

This book describes 150 RV living tips that will ensure you have a truly magnificent RV experience. The tips are universal and simple to apply; but how much these tips go towards improving your life while on the go will surprise you.

To make this guide a fun and effective read, we shall segment the tips into three sections: RV living, RV traveling, and having fun as you embark on an RV adventure of a lifetime.

Thanks again for ordering this book, I hope you enjoy it!

Chapter 1: RV Living

Travelling in an RV is an exciting experience; however, because RV living demands, at its very core, being on the go, you may miss some of the things you would experience if you were living in a stationary home. In this section, we shall look at RV living tips that should make the experience exciting:

1. When purchasing an RV, go through the motions

You can stand in the shower, lie in the bed and sit on the RV toilet. Do not take this for granted.

2. Bigger is not always better; but if you are keen on comfort then consider it

The RV you choose will be your home. While, you do not need over 37 feet of RV space, if you are keen on comfort, consider an RV longer than 37 foot.

3. As far as RV living goes, less is more

One of the bigger mistakes you will make is splashing on a huge RV. Not only does it complicate travel, the larger space is also harder to manage.

4. When buying a tow vehicle, bigger is always better

When buying a tow vehicle, always go for the biggest engine. This will make your RV life much easier.

5. Consider buying an aerodynamic RV

An aerodynamic RV is superb in that it will save you a lot of money you would have spent on fuel over its lifetime.

6. Beware of purchasing RVs in vacant lots

Never buy an RV from an empty lot no matter how good the deal sounds.

7. Get solar power

Several solar panels spread on your RV's top will make an absolute difference. Solar power will be all you need for every power related need and will truly make your RV a home.

8. Online RV communities will be one of the best things you discover. Sign up to your nearest one now

Online RV communities have a constant stream of fresh tips geared towards improving your RV living experience. It also feels great when you know you are part of a community that enjoys a similar passion.

9. **Having a cell phone is important. You can also use prepaid phone cards**

Being on the move so often, your communication needs will be higher than normal because the distance demands constant communication with your loved ones, which is why cell phones or phone cards are an essential must have.

10. **When night temperatures get low, use a portable space heater to ease pressure on your overworked propane powered furnace**

Furnaces use a lot of propane, which may make RV living a bit expensive. A portable space heater will ease this cost, and the pressure placed on your propane-powered furnace.

11. **Install an effective water filter on your RV**

Without a water filter, life in the RV will be very rough simply because water from unverified and unsafe places is a breeding ground for disease.

12. **Do not dive into a full-fledged RV life if you cannot properly back up your RV**

Reversing your RV is very important. To become better at backing up, practice endlessly in a parking lot that is empty until you are sure you can comfortably reverse your RV.

13. High beams are not as important as you think

When traveling in foggy conditions, high beams are nothing more than decorations. Too many RV travelers tend to exaggerate their importance. If you insist on fitting them, that is okay but do not feel compelled to have them: they are not a necessity.

14. Water leaks greatly disrupt RV living

A likely cause of water leaks is worn rubber seals around your doors and windows. When you notice a leak, drop everything, and promptly fix it.

15. Follow the "two shoes" rule

You ought to have and use two pairs of shoes at any one time. Use one of the pairs outside the RV, and the other within the RV. This will be helpful, especially in instances where you have to venture outside the RV during muddy conditions.

16. Plastic covers are assets: have plenty of them

During heavy rain, an 8'x10' cover will come in handy to cover your supplies; it will be useful as ground cover placed under blankets for impromptu picnics, or even as a makeshift tablecloth.

17. If you are experiencing roof leaks, the first suspect should be the air conditioner!

Double-check your air conditioner bolts and seals. If tightening is necessary, immediately get to it.

18. During cold weather, use the same cold weather maneuvers you use at home

Place weather strip around your doors, add some rugs for better insulation, and consider having heavier curtains and drapes.

19. Good old WD-40

You do not have to go for WD-40 alone. Any other oil penetrative, water-displacing spray will make your RV life better.

20. Bring along a polarity tester

Using a polarity tester before you plug in the electrical cord will tell you if your hookup is working properly, which will keep you from electric shocks or worse.

21. Install an answering machine in your RV

If you are worried about missing incoming calls, consider installing an answering machine. Installing one will help you communicate easily.

22. Consider PVC tubes

PVC tubing is inexpensive and an ultimately safe way to transport your fishing poles.

23. Be serious about plumbing

Treat your plumbing system kindly. FOr instance, apart from cleaning, you should always purchase biodegradable toilet paper.

24. Do not fit electric steps on your RV

Electric steps lead to repeatedly bruised shins.

25. Clean your RV's engine once a year

Cover every sensitive component such air intake, the filter, the distributor, the fuse box, etc. Warm up your engine to loosen any gunk, but do not allow your engine to get hot, and then wrap up by spraying with degreaser.

26. Always have aluminum foil

Aluminum foil has a million and one uses. From wrapping food to acting as an insulator extraordinaire; thus, it is almost unacceptable to live in an RV without aluminum foil.

27. Regularly Clean your RV

Oxidation of the RV's rubber roof, best shown by the presence of ugly streaks, is usually unavoidable. However, keeping the roof clean will lessen these effects. Start by removing all the debris on the roof and using clean water to wash the roof. Choose whatever cleaning agent you fancy and follow the cleaning instructions. Perform this cleaning exercise at least three times every year. For rips and tears, stock a patch kit in your RV.

28. Invest in a slide topper

A slide topper is a handy way to keep moisture and debris off the slide-out rooms; thus, have one.

29. Fit your RV with comfort elements

The RV doubles up as your home. Spend some money on electronic mirrors, on cruise control, and a good stereo.

30. Rustproof your RV

You can rustproof the chassis by undercoating it at a specialty shop or using an after-market spray. Either way, rustproofing will keep the RV's foundation in proper working order.

31. Understand RV living is minimalistic living

Accept that the RV shall not have every convenience present in a regular home. As you embark on RV living, you will have to live without some things.

32. Invest in dark carpeting

With a carpet installed, you will enjoy staying barefoot within the RV. Dark carpeting will also demand less cleaning sessions.

33. Before or after you park your RV for a longer period, thoroughly clean it

Steam clean your carpet and then launder every clothing item, blanket, and towel. Clean every drawer, and if necessary, spray for bugs. Clean your furnace, the AC, and the fan filters.

34. Become a proficient map reader

Every RV traveler, including you must know the various ins and outs of map reading.

35. Always have duct tape

Count the number of times you use duct tape in your regular home in a single week. Now, multiply the figure you get by a hundred. What you come up with is an approximate number of times you will use duct tape as you adventure in your RV.

36. The Importance of the Surge Protector

Surge protectors will offer economical insurance against issues like power spikes. Power spikes are often hard on pricey onboard equipment in your RV.

37. Be smart and use things wisely

It is a good habit to conserve your resources. For instance, do not allow your water to run for no reason.

38. Ensure you have rubber gloves

A box of rubber gloves will be useful when you are dealing with sewer hookups as well as the dump station.

39. Before you purchase, have a walk through with the salesperson

Before you leave the dealership with your new RV, arrange a walk through with the salesperson. Make sure every appliance, utility, and every function in the new RV is in pristine working condition.

40. Your cockpit can never be too comfortable

Of all the places in your RV, the cockpit needs to receive the most attention. Make sure it is as comfortable as possible: you will spend a lot of time there.

41. Mud flaps may be old school, but they are necessary

A set of mud flaps will ensure minimal debris in your vehicle.

42. Carry paper plates

Partially folded paper plates make for easily usable funnels.

43. Keep extension cords short

If you need an extension cord for electric hookups or any hookup type, use as short a length as possible. The longer the cord distance is, the more the voltage drop shall be.

44. Garbage Has No Place in your RV

Trash aboard your RV is an unnecessary hassle. One of the ways to deal with unnecessary trash is to transfer foods such as cereals and meats from their unnecessarily oversized packaging into modest packages. You should also consider re-using and recycling paper.

45. Who said standing on top of your RV is cool?

Unless you have a bucket of soapy water and a mop in your hands, it beats all sense why you should stand on top of your rig.

46. Furnace 101

Occasionally check the outside of the furnace for soot. Soot is always a sign of faulty functioning. Clean and then vacuum your unit as is necessary. Check your hoses for any kinks and replace as is needed. Have a pro inspect your system at least once every year.

47. When you stop to wash your RV, do it in the shade

The sun, while quickening the RV drying process, also quickens the drying time of the cleaning agents you use. The follow up waxing procedure is then too much work.

48. Incorporate an onboard timer

The onboard timer for RV lights will chase away potential thieves. This concept is similar to the set up you have in a regular home.

49. Install handrails in the entryway of your RV

This will help avoid falls.

50. Two hoses are better than one!

Stocking a couple of 25-foot long hoses is a lot better than having a single 50-foot long hose.

51. Install a radio in your RV!

While the radio chatter may often be irritating and a little crude, it has its uses. The radio will be a valuable resource for information such as upcoming traffic, the weather, and even area recommendations. Additionally, a radio will ease the monotony of driving.

52. Do not stock fruits and veggies

Fruit and vegetables from roadside stands will always taste better than what you have in your RV fridge or freezer.

53. Do not set up a bed in the cab-over area

In case you insist on arguing with this invaluable logic, know that no one above 13 years likes sleeping in that space.

54. Take care of your RV insurance

Be sure that the RV insurance covers your trips abroad.

55. Have a higher deductible

The first step is to be a good driver. The second step is to know that a good driver will carry a higher deductible on his/her insurance. The third step is to act on what you know.

56. Invite your friends

Travelling with family and friends makes the RV experience better.

57. While you may be on the move, do not eat as if you are on the run

Do you want your poultry, hamburgers, and steak to taste better? Let your cooked meats sit and stew for a few minutes before you serve. Cooking using high heat will force the juices inward, which will make the food less tasty. Waiting for a few minutes before delving in will make a big difference in the taste.

58. Make sure your RV is level when parked

For your RV's refrigerator to work properly, your RV must be level. Thus, leveling your RV is of utmost importance.

59. Always have an emergency kit

Create your emergency kit and place it in a safe outside compartment. Your first aid kit must be inclusive of first aid equipment, pencils and a paper sheaf, a flashlight, and a disposable camera (the latter is for capturing any accident scenes). Compile a list of names such as lawyer, doctor, insurance agent, etc. as well as any medications you are currently using. Then, hope that you will never have to open this kit.

60. Replace your wipers

Change the windshield wipers as necessary or at least once a year.

61. Use an electronic awning

Once you use an electronically deployed awning, you will never look back.

Chapter 2: RV Traveling

In this section, we shall outline invaluable tips that will make traveling in your RV easier:

62. If you do not know your RV's weight, chances are, it is overloaded

Occasionally weigh your RV to find out how much your RV weighs while fully loaded. Here, RV size is a factor; still, you can easily tell if your RV is overloaded. An overloaded RV is an accident in waiting.

63. As you travel, use two carpet samples

Use two carpet samples; one placed at the entry steps' base and the other at the top, will keep dirt as well as moisture away from the RV's interior.

64. Note your RVs exterior height

Write your RVs exact height (and do not forget to add its A/C) and GVWR and then proceed to place this measurement in your cockpit. This is important because it will help you ensure you do not exceed the RV's weight capability and perhaps risk an accident while driving under overpasses.

65. Do not drive more than 500 miles a day

If anything, driving 400 miles is a little excessive. There is wear and tear to consider. If you push 400 miles, your rig will wear and tear faster.

66. If you have a pet, travel with him/her: there is no better experience than traveling with your pet

Pets are good company, especially if the bond between you and your pet is a strong one. Even when you have a partner, traveling in an RV can be lonely especially when you have to drive for many hours. Thus, a pet makes a great monotony breaker.

67. Give your pet some attention

Pick up after your pet, keep your pet leashed (for dogs), and take your pet out for a daily walk. The occasional cookie or treat will not hurt either.

68. Although a pet is fun, set hard and fast RV rules for your pet!

Here is a gem of advice: if you allow your dog into your RV bed just once, the dog will be there until the day he/she dies.

69. Fill your tanks at all times

As an RV owner, avoid, as much as possible, idling in rush hour traffic with your tanks only a quarter full. Imagine what would happen if your RV ran out of gas in thick rush hour traffic. The thought of pushing that RV as other motorists chip in with a symphony of hoots is a nightmare.

70. RVs are not only good for camping in the woods. If you can travel to a beach, go for it

It will be good to experience contrasting places: campsites and beach areas. The different conditions will greatly improve your RV experience.

71. Be careful with medication; some medication causes sleepiness, which may hinder safe driving

Carefully read medication labels and determine if any of the medication you are using, causes drowsiness. All it takes is a few seconds to read medication labels; these few seconds could save your life.

72. Before you back up into campsites, get off the RV and look around

You are not looking to cause other campers accidents or damage your RV; thus, always look around.

73. If you cannot see him, he cannot see you

If you are behind an RV with the intention of aiding the backing up process, if you cannot see the driver, rest assured the driver cannot see you and does not know where you are.

74. Visit your nation's capital

Why is this necessary? For one, even though it looks unlikely, some of the most thriving RV communities call your nation's capital their home base.

75. Before you even think of moving, walk around your RV

Check all your lights and signals. Examine your tires for any wear and tear and measure the pressure. Double check your trailer hookups, the dollies, the tow bars, or any items that may fall of and break once you start moving.

76. Slow down

Yet another gem here for you: if you were truly in such a hurry, you should have left yesterday. Slow down and enjoy the ride.

77. Avoid traveling during the day

Hot-weather driving is usually hard on your RV. Travel in the morning and late in the afternoon. These times also have less traffic anyways.

78. Stopping your RV is tricky business

It will usually take your RV a distance equal to a fifth of the length of a football field to come to a complete stop; thus, make your calculations when you want to stop the RV.

79. Be careful when reversing your RV

As professional instructor, Dick Reed likes to say, the valid spelling of "reverse" is "S-L-O-W".

80. Make as many stops as you can

Stop at any roadside diners and any place that has the word "EAT" highlighted in neon. The more stops you make, the more you can "top up" and thus, be more comfortable.

81. Interact with campsite folk as much as possible

If you want some information or do not know something, it will not hurt to ask those in the next campsite. Often, campers will be glad to help out fellow campers.

82. The backup monitor

While backup monitors are wonderful, they are costly. If you are interested in buying one, ensure the camera functions in the dark. A backup monitor that becomes useless after the sun goes down limits travel.

83. When dealing with hills, maintain gear consistency

When tackling a particularly tough ascent, go downhill with the same gear you went up.

84. Perform regular checkups

In all honesty, you do not need someone to constantly remind you to check the RV's LP gas, smoke detector, and carbon monoxide detector, do you?

85. If possible, travel with a copilot

It does not matter if you are traveling with your spouse or a friend. Teach your copilot how to drive and backup the RV, and ask him or her take the wheel often. Why is this necessary? Think of it this way: supposing you, the main driver, got hurt or sick, what would happen?

86. Do the smart thing and avoid traveling in an overloaded RV

Traveling in an overloaded RV is not worth the risk. The extra weight accelerates wear and tear. In addition, you can bet that overloading your RV will cost you your insurance claim. Now you see why it is not worth the risk.

87. If possible, visit every national park

Why do this? Well, why not do this?

88. Maintain positive relations with your copilot

One of the greatest tips is to never engage your copilot in fights or negatively heated discussions. If you are keen on having a pleasant journey, you need to keep your partner happy.

89. Before commencing travel, perform the Prevost bus test

If you feel uncomfortable and cramped in a standard 40 foot Prevost bus, then RV travel is just not for you.

90. Keep a roll of quarters handy

You can always keep them in the shower kit. This will be helpful when you travel and the bathrooms you have to use insist on pay-per-use. You will never believe just how vital these quarters are until you try to get change for a 20-dollar bill with nothing on but a robe and wet slippers.

91. Have a few words with the campground owner

It is always a good idea to have a word with the campground owner; you will be surprised at how much you can learn from them.

92. Get up and move

If you are the owner of a functional RV, why remain at a place you dislike?

93. Take care of travel lists

Compile and then laminate a couple of basic lists: the first one will be setting up the campsite, and the other will be breaking camp. This way, you will never find yourself driving off with the antenna up.

94. Do not pack and travel; inform your loved ones

Make sure that your family members have the names as well as addresses of the places you will stay for the next few weeks.

95. Does your state or your country have a wooded reserve? If so, visit it

A good example in the US is Maine. Visit and learn the history there. Wooded areas tend to have interesting histories.

96. Incorporate Sway Bars

If your RV does not have sway bars, you will have a hard time containing your RV's body roll motions.

97. Making camp reservations

When you are making your campground reservations, take several minutes to detail the exact site you want. If you fancy being in close proximity to the bathroom or say, the swimming pool or if you require fewer trees because your RV is large, inform the camp management in advance. Even if all you want is the prettiest place on the site, do not be shy.

98. Carry along a compass

While having a GPS is nice, nothing beats a compass's effectiveness at preventing moving around in aimless circles.

99. It is not camping unless there are s'mors

This means you must make room for that Boy Scout camping stuff you have conditioned yourself against; you never know when you will need it.

100.   Take your tires very seriously

Do not mess around with the RV tires. Thoroughly and regularly, inspect your tires and once you notice the very first signs of a worn tread, replace your tires. It is also wise to buy your tires in pairs. Check your tire pressure before long trips.

Chapter 3: Having Fun in an RV

RV travel and living is an adventure; as such, it should be fun. This section of the guide will look at invaluable ways to make your RV adventure fun, enjoyable, and above all, adventurous:

Play Fun Indoor Games

101.   Play cards in your RV

This one is a no brainer. Cards take up almost no space. The best thing about cards is that the number of games you can play is limitless.

102.   Play Yahtzee

This game is a must have for every RV owner. With Yahtzee, you roll your dice and try your luck. You get to score points using various combos of the die, which is inclusive of straights, three & four and the ever-elusive Yahtzee.

103.   Play Monopoly

The beauty of this game is that regardless of whether you are two or more, you will have limitless, intense fun.

104. Play LCR

While LCR is a tiny game, it is a lot of fun. You will mostly be rolling dice, aching to gamble, and it will be more than enough to keep you occupied.

105. Carry along a Jenga kit

What is that saying again, old is gold? It rings particularly true here. This game is quite fun. Pieces are stacked high on each other and every player has to take out a piece without knocking over the structure. This very simple model is so much fun that some RV owners consider it the only game they need to bring along.

106. Play Apples to Apples

This lovely party game has two card decks: a description deck and a "things" deck. One player draws a description deck while the partner tries to match this by drawing a "things" card. This game is quite mentally challenging.

107. Play cards against humanity

The first thing you ought to know is that this is not a game for kids. Many adults have described it a version of Apples to Apples.

108.   Play Scrabble

Just how much of a word guru are you? Yet another old game that is fun to play.

109.   Play board games

Depending on just how many young ones you bring along on your RV adventure, you will need several board games. You cannot go wrong with Candy-land, Hungry, Hungry Hippos, and Life!

110.   Carry a Chessboard

Only adults will truly have fun with this one. Nevertheless, although slow paced and deep thought stirring, chess is a lot of fun.

111.   Play old Corn Hole

Have you ever tried pitching horseshoes? If no, you ought to try it but not before you try corn hole. It is a lot similar, except instead of using horseshoes and poles, you use beanbags and boards.

112.   Bring Jarts along

This is quite a fun game to play.

113.   Play Frisbee/Baseball/Basketball/Football

What is more fun than throwing something back and forth, in a competitive atmosphere?

114.   Bring along a GPS for some geo-catching

This is a favorite for many families traveling in an RV. All you need is a small GPS and proceed to find a small container hidden in the park by following given coordinates. While the catch does not really hold anything of value, the hunt is a lot of fun.

115.   Play some Kanjam

Kanjam is another must have game. The game is a version of corn-hole; however, instead of throwing beanbags, you throw a Frisbee at a plastic cylinder.

116.   Play Washers

Washers is a game that combines multiple elements from several games including horseshoes. This is one of the RV games you can play with teams.

117.   Play Soccer

Soccer is incredibly cheap to set up and play. All you need is a soccer ball, a pump, and to set up makeshift goalposts.

118.   Bike Races

Bring along some bikes and engage in some biking competition. Biking is an ingenious way to give your legs a workout while having fun.

119.   Carry along some spelunking gear

If you are going to visit an area that has many caves, this will be a lot of fun. You can turn it into a game by competing to see who will discover the most things. However, before you venture into the caves, it is advisable to seek assistance from an experienced guide.

120.   Play Hide and Seek

There is some magic in hide and seek. No matter how old you get, it will always be fun.

Fun Indoor Activities For When You Are Stuck In Your RV

121.   Read Books and Magazines

You do not have to attach a particular order to this one. If anything, the more random the stuff you read, the better.

122. Read aloud to each other

Unfortunately, not very many of us do this one often. Other than being a lot of fun, reading aloud improves your reading skills.

123. Bring along a painting kit

Painting is a superb fun activity because it needs very little space and knowing you are creating art is a lot of fun.

124. Knit and sew

Knitting and sewing are fun and constructive activities you can do.

125. Bring along portable devices for movies

Portable DVDs are cheap enough these days. Laptops, while costing slightly more, are also cheap enough to have and carry along.

126. Play games on electronic devices

You don't need to carry along too many electronic devices; your phone is good enough for this.

127.   Tell each other made up stories

Push your story telling creativity and see just how creative you can be.

128.   Snuggle

Just snuggle with your loved ones.

129.   Take impromptu naps

Other than being fun, naps invigorate you in a way few other things can.

130.   Daydream

It is a lot of fun to lean back in your RV and allow your mind to wander.

Fun Night Time RV Activities

131.   Create shadow puppets in your RV

Bonus points for you if you can use your fingers and shadows to create some creative figures.

132.   Take nighttime walks

Something about nightly walks makes them so special. Perhaps it is the solitude and peace as the world sleeps. However, remember to exercise caution and be safe.

133.   Play Flashlight Tag

Yet another activity kids and adults alike can enjoy. All you need is a flashlight and willing people.

134.   Play Hide and Seek in the dark

One activity that is more fun than hide and seek is hide and seek in the dark.

135.   Go for a midnight swim

This one is so unconventional that thinking about it spells instant fun. While everyone is sleeping, you can enjoy yourself in the pool.

136.   Study stars

If you have a small telescope, this one is truly fascinating.

137. Shoot off fireworks

Before you proceed with this one, make sure you are familiar with the State's laws on fireworks. Having to pay a fine when all you were trying to do is have some fun is no fun.

138. Tell ghost stories

No matter what they tell you, everyone enjoys being a little scared in the dark. If anything, it helps you appreciate present company.

139. Play truth or dare

This one will forever remain a classic.

140. Play a guitar in your rig

Regardless of whether you are proficient at playing the instrument or not, it is immense fun to strum guitar strings.

Fun Driving Activities

141. Sing along to your stereo

The most fun thing about singing along to your music system is that it creates the illusion that your voice is just as good as the singer's is. The second most fun thing about singing along to your stereo is that it is fun.

142.   Listen to motivational CDs

Nothing gets you more energized than listening to a motivational CD as you drive. With a good motivational CD in the stereo, you want to drive forever and journeys will seem shorter.

143.   Learn a new language while driving

Get into the habit of listening to some audio and trying to learn a new language as you drive. The results after only a few weeks will amaze you.

144.   Listen to symphonies

Symphonies are soothing and magical; you will not notice how much long the journey has been.

145.   Listen to an audio bible

If you are religious, listen to an audio version of the bible. If nothing, you will finish the entire book faster than most people manage to.

Relaxing In RV Activities

146.   Bring along a rocking chair

It is immensely relaxing and fun to rock back and forth in a rocking chair, especially in an RV. The fact that only a few do it gives it a special feel.

147. Listen to nature

Lean back, put away your headphones and iPod, and listen to the sounds of nature. You will have fun and feel at peace.

148. Star Gaze

Pull back your RV's curtains and look at the sky. Try to see how many stars you can count before you lose track.

149. Watch trees

There is something wondrous about the slow rhythm and perpetual motion trees have in the wind.

150. Immerse yourself in the tub

By immersing yourself in the tub, you stay clean, relax, and enjoy yourself. This sounds like a phenomenal deal.

Conclusion

Thank you again for buying this book!

This book has given you 150 tips to make your life in your RV exciting, safe, adventurous, and fun. Put these tips in action now for an overall, better RV experience.

Finally, if you enjoyed this book, would you be kind enough to leave a review for this book?

Thank you and good luck!

John

Made in the USA
San Bernardino, CA
18 December 2016